Icarus Redux

Matt Santateresa

Icarus Redux

The **Mansfield** Press

National Library of Canada Cataloguing in Publication

Santateresa, Matt, 1950-
Icarus Redux / Matt Santateresa.

Poems.
ISBN 1-894469-12-7

I. Title.

PS8587.A3739I33 2003 C811'.54 C2003-901503-3
PR9199.3.S224I33 2003

Cover and Text design by Tim Hanna
Cover photo courtesy of Magma Photo
Author photo by Paula Belina

The publication of *Icarus Redux* has been generously supported by
The Canada Council for the Arts and
the Ontario Arts Council.

The Canada Council for the Arts since 1957 | Le Conseil des Arts du Canada depuis 1957

Ontario Arts Council
Conseil des Arts de l'Ontario

Mansfield Press Inc.
25 Mansfield Avenue
Toronto, Ontario, Canada
M6J 2A9
Publisher Denis De Klerck
www.mansfieldpress.net

Printed in Canada

Contents

The Light Dreams Have

Icarus Redux

Now and Elsewhere

The Light Dreams Have

Eyelashes

A baby spider, red and miniscule,
lands and manages across the white page
to escape this mortal nib,
    reminds me of her eyelashes, gossamer
and like first words in fall from elementary school
teacher's lips, finely transported to a blackboard
in virgin cursive chalk lines
    Miss Andersen, Miss Hughes, Miss Allen
words that lingered after daylight hours

eyelashes flick, hers, when
    eyes nictitate with pleasure until sleep and her
rapid eye movements dart in oblivion

Sprung Spring

Gulls mimic a master's voice
and laugh
Morning fog dissipates
on a need to know basis
Differences coalesce as we speed along
spilling milk and
seamen leave harbours with persistent
flow, graffiti reconnoitres corners
of a building, engineers lonely
and passive as time takes
its atoll, atomic time
brushes everything knowable
and beyond truth itself
when those were the days
our skin thin as airplane wings
our phantom limbs ached
to reach a god

Visitation: Up Here

Television is a non sequitur up here
    any tool, machine that does not
fix survival or clear a view
    for that savage sense of power
is useless
    but what breeds is silence
luminous or not, green or dark
    it shines with long meditation
beyond wordsworthian words and keatsian views
    and weal and reach of beauty
that breaks with nails hammering these keys
    to build a passing dream
though perfectly alive, wave as cars
    roll past this figure in a timely landscape

a pedestrian standing on a street corner, waits
    as metallic vapours luft through heart
and lungs of socialist desires and disappointments
    engineered awake all night with demons
unexorcised sitting on momentary shoulders, then

a sudden bird has launched itself unknowing
    against a pane of glass that reflects his forest and
lands broken on the grass struggling
    to fly and eventually does as I approach more feared
than loved
    though knowing
the quiet, up here, defines a near future

Woods

A mind is movement enough
where woods' daunting edges
lapse into mystery
call from lambent clearings with
voices whose history is war
and camouflage, spirits who
swell and dwell in magic; centaurs,
satyrs, maenads, calling for a return
to green parties laughing over duff
and love bushed as a hind flees
from our noise, a dignified thing
no less

but faster still a mind's superfluous will
to conduct its imaginary work fully clothed
and hearing a trill from inside a room's
screen and magnified light breaking
a Rorschach into motion and
who sees in a static wall
Socrates build a forum from leaves
for question and answer periods
arise animated hints for futures
mapping galaxies

can be seen from here
through the shade and light-fissured woods
as quick as something said
and gone

Shock

To claim the empire for building
    clear the land first
chainsaw with trembling hands a two HP
    engine snapping annual rings
whole ancestral grounds
    make it smooth as steel
and then a castle from which
    an enemy army approaching is visible
or a lover's anticipation galloping toward
    sweet naked wills. . .

but here, it is anonymous, the purchased trees
    and purchased land; rocky, mossy,
a perfect cottage from this vista of pond and sunset
    so here the cuts begin, trees fall, breaking
cracking as they climb down in a rattling sound

    a crow calls, intermittent and flies
across this chest of wordless shock
    black as a fallen bole
last seen its glittering wings

    awakening to white sheets, these hands settling on
nothing, first see a white frock, unreadable badge, a smile
    a moveable thumb
intensive care is my room

but not a crow in sight
    a moth darkly sits on a white wall
and breathing again begin to belabour a point, that shock
    limned there, by a dawn, its silent unmoveable wings
sitting unsought, in a combustible light.

Night Above the Trees, Butter My Sleepmask, Please

So it will never stay on
    as the pouring rain augments a wooden roof
and hauling the thing off
    stop to listen
from a dream of floodwaters and mudslides
    through these mainspring genes as green cleavers
whistled through perimeter sleeves that billowed
    gratuitous it seemed as I ducked and danced and
not one cut by those leaves
    though some sightseer to all this
now unbandaged and this flesh white
    breathing lighter than imagined, looking around
hearing rain resonate its immortal presence
    see the gray mask, limp,
its own dissembled verb, instigate nothing
    but a round stored world of posthumous
pictures, maelstrom of black starless pines, hopeless
    night water
there on a pine table it sits useless as a poem
    waiting to take hold of head and frame
with wild interventions to resound with sportive
    meanings —
butter my sleepmask, please
    let it unwind, throw away my backups
in drawers, under carpets, hidden
    and obvious, the ones implanted from birth
waiting for use in conversation's lull, in naps through
garden walks, a snooze through mindless moments
    listening for nothing, waiting for nothing
to come around and take on its black rounded view
butter my sleepmask, please
    let it slip from these hands
bury its doom in feral woods, its moon, its dark, its need
    to cover more and more
its constant imploring,
    put me on! put me on!

The Light Dreams Have

she sleeps curled
on the roof rapt
in a cradle of
night music

the leaves are sailing
rustling canvas
lufting hard like bed sheets
across the seas
to Morovia at midnight
across Alps' sudden thaw
to imagination

in the dream there
is no reason
as a raven plies to
ask how she
found herself there
sleeping awake, nuzzling
cold air, a natal position
as if for birth to prepare

we are in this light, you
and I, that breaks open
each day in a sky
where you are towering

I dream for
those atop this roof
on nights with invisible
wings in a light dreams have

and though these eyes
are closed, you are here
in full sight, speaking
with me in this full light

yet I cannot fall asleep
and topple from this place
onto the hard earth below
that calls me over and over
through rain and snow,
pleading with me to leave and

latch onto the ground, where it wants
us all to go.

So Far

you are indistinguishable and dispensable
as millions who continue
melancholic or in utter joy
with impulsive sprees to buy
and love
somewhere a mother, a father
lust or desire, made you
suffering becomes you, brushes
you constantly as continuous lineage
like an old river
its thin soul burning

Still Life

To date
an arpeggio sun can be heard
and I can still speculate
on beauty, death
a restful life
in potential sits prepared

keys in a lump on a table,
nothing locked in a trunk, no gelnite

scissors yawn, left open, no stabbing
to perform

a candle has no wick to ignite a war
but stands

like this portable radio, its antenna
my heart missing in action

Pastoral

Like Prufrock I pull sweat pants up
To my knees and divulge secrets to myself
I had no inkling existed at this point in time. It is brazen
To be alive with antiquity dead
And pursue dreams still
As clouds scud, their shapes like sheep
The time to forget has arrived
A sole telephone booth I a saviour
My 911 I shall not want
And the valley here is steely-jawed industrial
Having no shepherds.

Sparrow

Keatsian. Diminutive sound buried
in brush and through traffic's bassline noise
hear your high spirit call
and sit lower down in an unkempt
park at a black table and bench
to scan slight women taking dogs for walks
scolding their rebellious pees on flimsy
tulips about to, scoop
sparrow, prodigious in numbers
like the Chinese who eat you, an aphrodisiac
our temporality too slow for you
appearing to have no limits at all.

A Shlitz and cigars. Leave Donne
and St. Paul at home along with courtesans
Wyatt and Sydney on the sill
here are the torn screen doors, telephone
poles aslant, no mothers' overweaning
dependence of Oxbridge boys. Sparrows'
dusty plumage shimmers in the sun
as they dart and bandy among triplexes
squabbling.

Sound

A moth flutter
    inside a lampshade
circles warm light
    bumps silence and exits
to darkness
    and re-enters
the shade its boundary, fixed,
    yearns to be an instinct
of light, a moon say
    and continues its dance
to the sound of its birth

Refuge

Those encyclopedic ceiling fans
of the last 50-odd years that feed
hot settings of the movie *Casablanca* or where
Aiken or Crane or Dickey
would write drunk on
voices before they
disappear, life itself being rails
toward epiphany

Trees outside hold referendums
in a breeze, fanning,
squirrels don't fantasize
their lives as birds
or read St. Augustine for affirmation
happiness is not
a question in this kingdom
of survival, a creator
has no value at all
how happy can we be
because of knowledge and choices
to forget a bitter childhood, a lover,
a friend deadened to friendship
or happily remember a summer
of refuge under a tree's loquacious life
organized so frightfully
as to be encyclopedic

though this room is a mess of years
remnants
to turn and return to
from absence or mindfulness
but see where branches diverge
say nothing with grace and
in a wide blue yonder
the green turns and turns
cutting out more and more
words

Poetry

Colt .45* is my Lethe
and hearing the wine flow delectable
as a dream on warm breezes
into miles of poetic diction recurrent
loves who expressed influential
poems memorized as dysfunctional parents
beat each other to a pulp
or a crude and cruel lover outsized every
possible thought with words
disastrous as institutional foreplay
or earthquakes
knowing its seismic end
words committed to memory
cry and sob as deep
as Coleridge at night hearing
calves lowing at nine
or thereabouts
sprung with poetry
its sovereign state

**Beer brewed in Detroit, Michigan.*

Woods II

A mind is movement enough
    where woods' daunting edge calls
in those limbic clearings with post-mortem charm
    where history fights its wars, civil and otherwise,
eros and thanatos
    collide in continuity, where spirits dwell and swell
with magic centaurs, satyrs, maenads
    to hear green calls and cries and possibly a hind
in quick escape
    fast enough on the brain's superfluous cells
that connect to reason
    and leave these words to accumulate
for years of thinking and rethinking one thing or another
    one grace or another
these moving Rorschach figures you recall

like that Socrates diorama you saw in the blots
    his last forum among the leaves
words plainly state his side, movement of his robes, his pacing
    concern for reason as he spots, you'll recall
fleeing into trees' fissured shades
    and evaporate, something, something

quick as speaking words like
    a mind is movement enough

House

He says the birds haven't a clue
they come in full tilt, nothing
to tip them off, though God's given them
acute eyesight, hearing that could home in
on a troubled mate miles away
and bam! Smack into the second
floor window, some are simply dazed
and fall on the patio, shaken, rebound
and resume flight
others are killed by the reflection
of familiar trees, grove
sparrow, woodpecker, thrush, no particular
species escape the illusion
the window creates, and like us
can lose their lives in the process.

Giving Flowers to ESL Teachers

Seeing you through the window
white bouquet in my hand —
there you are in a numbing classroom,
full of wonderful accents,
teaching English as another language
to others who want to be pilots,
better housewives, executives, bus drivers
and want to return home
shivering with salvation and conjugation
landing a new vision of themselves
in hopeful English terms,
flying home in pure translucence, with see-through hearts
that grow as some plant through its chromatic phases
across landscapes of China, Mexico, Japan, Russia,
all countries that fill
with appropriate English tenses for ventures,
occupations and desires and you have them
wanting to take more courses
explaining the parts of language with chalk drawings
white meaningful arrows that flower and dovetail into shimmering
off jet's aluminum skins, city states, empires
of corruptible palms for markets, for raids and assaults
for black roses of ash and soot, for dreadful chapters
in the history of a nation held to ransom in letters of
broken headlines, in clipped phrases of perfect English
then again, who can be responsible for these lessons
in which you teach the trust of a grammar
its elements like rose petals
or the magic belly of a cheerleader, full money clip,
a beautiful voice in the head to behave in communication
of upright values and ideals — what can hold you culpable
if this language goes on to learn landmines or shrapnel, or a savage bug-love,
or like Deuteronomy a terrible, messed up language of vengeance,
a kill-switch mechanism,
dead stop of everything, you teach so beautifully not knowing
what or who will die or grow, loving them, loving the language they learn.

En Passant

As dreams take a turn toward death
I'm bolt upright at 3 am
sucking in air for life, a fear of
dying has every thought strangled

I awaken you for no other
reason than an escort to an emergency ward
companion, too
desperate with fear who presents
a way of knowing how alive I am
how dead Henry Fonda is hours ago
his voice on television
describes beavers on a nature show
and that is how I desire
but know how impossible
it would be to be remembered or not
forgotten, too

our talk was unexceptional
your solace, succor going unnoticed
buried in male imperfections
unable to put these thoughts together
at that time for you
a gasp with a wordless survival

it ended well
embrace and sleep, sweet
relapse of life, soft inhale
exhale, sleep
until
for real, no redress possible
nothing like you to absorb

night's final episode
only a reminiscent twinge
not epic proportions
a foregone seclusion that drives home
a final breath, rale.

I miss you already.

Searchlights

A nation of nostalgia
brims with golden oldies
that stretch back to, say,
a dance era, a peace
era, a snare of drums, sweet melancholies burning, devising to make
millions from Carnegie's tips, night
spots free love, a music
that widens its searchlight beam

so that you get a whiff of another world
to hijack moments away, stave off
responsibility with a strange security
of dim soldiers defending denial
along the coasts and borders

and so, glide back to salient good times
magic feet, magic hands,
to places behind her earlobe, her scapula
giving over to scores of love
strokes unimagined, again and again
because love is all there is
a searchlight that opens the dark.

A Time of Unimportance

I told you this is the country hydrangea white as sunlight
And beauty indifferent but beauty nonetheless
And you could be a fly that persists
To enter a hole in a window screen hearing the music
Of another side play
Like a nature poem that continuously babbles or rustles
And there you are wanting to enter its sanctum, wild
As Wyatt, as Will, only
You attribute too much city sense to its rhythms
Not enough reverence, too much cynicism from apartment sunsets
And can't quite assimilate into nature's existence
Let alone a poem, its persistence as green
And beautiful as you were taught in high school.
Crickets serenade trees or grass
Leaves appear to fibrillate into a future, or
Where nymphs, maenads lie in wait
Behind billboards like motorcycle cops begging
For you to accelerate toward your need to have more
Adrenaline pump up that dying tiger in you again
Naked in fields against laws heading lawless
Toward herds of fax machines, copiers, cellphones.
Down the road charging up with greenest warnings, O Moloch
The dearest minds are brilliant with numb definitions of you
On indifferent screens that a different beauty computerizes
As electric fences, alarms, ache to go off for pit bulls
To begin gnashing, chase you through grids of streets.
What training to kill is about, inhuman nature and
Finally that fly enters and proceeds to die to exit
Re-escape through the same rip in time, to find
In its compounded eyes
A thousand windows and suns and hydrangea,
Rolled up magazines.
You have been caught long enough in a room
As persistent as a poem aching to be written
And just as old as any music keeping insomniac nights
To get it right and besides I told you this is the country, relax,
Vacate your mind, everything is as unimportant here
As light is, you'll never have enough time to finish, anyway.

Rhythm and Archaeology

Clang
Clang
Nate is shaping a horseshoe
It turns everything else to silence
Said Bishop and Graves too
Je vous aime beaucoup
Turning round wondering what to do
My love for you is tres tres fort
Rhythm that starts from an atavistic core
Rivers that edify in slipstream sleep
Sounds that ageless emerge and steep
Continue past lineage and longstanding staples
Of every possible notion and constancy of opals
What archaeologies make of shards resounds
Like river's repeated tolls, a spirit sounds
In anvil and oar, Aeolian harp, elliptic
Longingly, lovingly mortal

Icarus Redux

If Truth Be Known

His wings caught on a waterwheel off Samos
And repeatedly turned for days on end until
A farmer spotted a curious shape glistening and
Approached to find wet feathers and a contraption
Of sorts and wood soaked and malleable.
Retrieving it he placed it in his oxcart for further review.

In his barn, this alien thing was perplexing, no technology
That he knew could figure this out, though the wings and
Their dusty wet aroma was familiar, all other premises or
Possibilities the farmer drew were blank, to no conclusion
And so became the work of devils.

This encapsulates a picture of thinking back then. Knowledge
Limited to a few, all the rest worried about yokes, seeds, bait
And grazing land, whatever requirements built survival and
Repetition of formulae and ritual reaped over
And over. In between a community celebrated with songs
In between their births and deaths.

Some nameless face in fathoms cradled in silence
Dreaming out loud.

Longing in a Panoramic View

Staring out like a dog, flying nowhere above
A precipice
An outcrop of Athens, Rome, Antioch, etc.
Changes and now pauses
In an atoll of sorts gathering more coral, algae,
Under layers that plumb good as limestone
Hold herbal shops, organic arrays
Soothe missionary work, real estate
Glues gods together for afterlives

Ole Christendom comes in chainmail and dice
Builds desert cities and hearths bright with prayers
Home a friendly cockle for children's toys like
Clay soldiers, whose arms and heads end under
A sofa's sprung spring

And those romantic geographers who need
To escape war's intimate details to Antarctic visions blinding
Gloom and titanium white prayers unceasing, indifferent
Air a cold audacity to breathe in

Or seeing tropic's teal sea, aerofoil palms another
Worldly copyright, trees mad with fragrance, voluptuous
Sound from sun's niche to chameleon's sand-cloyed skin

Nothing beats from here in wind and tree
Looking out over these cement, glass and steel nests
Shackles and tons, uproaring signs to rivers and
Mountains that secrete a longing taken
Unfettered and for no other reason than far away
As the eye can see

Unplanned

Icarus knows a poet whose hexameter lines
Drive young women wild with limbic activity

This particular bard dives right into skeins
Of uncertainty with a vengeance, into light
Years of wilderness, much against the current
Trend of adventure and epic, his rhythms recoil

Into the body of his work, so hypochondriac
He listens attentively to his arteries and skin,
Scrambles for sunscreen or inhales
Discoveries ad lib, keeps his robes clear
Of bird droppings, refreshes the albatross
Around his neck once a week to keep
Its eye glinting like a newly acquired
Ebony medallion.

Icarus sees in his eyes a kind of imprisonment
Of conscience, like tern eggs never hatched
Even though the poet could swim to the netherworld
And back, there was a need in his arms to throw
A nylon rope down from wherever he was and slip
Into the knot he tied and find intimate details of
Its composition or he would
Seek that wide open room to stray away in, mill
Around, glide over its Alps or after a five-thousand-foot
Dive into the sea taken down by sheer momentum
And spear a luminescent fish

And then resurface, scales of music dripping
As he soared back up, always the eye of a peregrine
Sleek doll eye with hungry focus, always
Shimmering, mercurial, fine tuned —

That's when Icarus wanted to fly
Leave his cells bookended with Bulfinch's

'Mythology,' the *OED* settled on shelves
Along with the *Elements of Style*.

That's when Icarus phoned his father
And said, "OK, let's do it, let's
Sweep the air!"

A Freeze-dried Notion of Beauty as Heard and Seen from a Barber's Chair

Icarus' old man has a shiny tanned face
And tells Icarus he loves to build things
While he cuts Icarus' hair on the balcony

Of their apartment. A summer sunlight shimmers
Off the Mediterranean. From nothing he says
Building what people love me to build the way

Bears' tongues drip with honey, bees madly buzzing
Around their heads. That love and desire so intense.
Icarus loves to hear this. He knows how bears

Steal into the night to hives hearing
Sweet inscrutable music in their ears. He loves it
When his father laughs and his eyes twinkle like

Bright waves. And his father says life is like a machine
That he builds that the world trusts completely
Until it breaks down, and then he says, death is like a repairman.

You call and explain what you think is wrong, only
To hear him say that there is nothing he can do, crucial parts
Have worn out, irreplacable parts, nothing can be fixed.

And yes, he knows everything was working perfectly yesterday
But that was yesterday. Now, Icarus smells the repairman
The haircut is nearly done and the fragrance of baby powder fills

His nostrils to the brain, as his father tamps some talc around his
Neck to cool scissor burn. It is done. His father hugs him
And tells him to fly a middle air between water and sun, and

Shakes the bib empty of Icarus' hair, then he laughs and spins
Icarus in his swivel chair, it moves 360 degrees and he sees
All is beauty around him, that he could not before

All the wilderness that meshes in a sweep and slowing down.
He sees the farmer struggle to straighten his plow, a fisherman
Reset a line with bait, a boat with sail like

A drying garment in a wind, and Icarus has an image of God
A form standing there gazing at the horizon, tanned, white bib in his hand
Barrel-chested, sun glancing off the blades.

Time and Space

This is our time and space, I imagine Minos says
To move lickety-split from grief
From past doldrums in warring that kept
Our uncles waist-deep in blood and ordered
Files along office windows. They smoked
As they typed reports, thrown second-hand into our faces.
This is our fantasy to deny all grief
That sends soldierless machines to bankroll
Enemy relief. An equilibrium, win-win
Situation booms what God finds indiscreet
Is no longer a sabotage that terrorists repeat,
But obscenity in fireballs that fly into our beliefs
And send reports, proposals, accounting sheets
Spreading like dust flying down our streets

This is our time and space, after all
And our love supplants our peace
So war can be made for safety's sake
And fashioned with grief
Equilibrium reigns our way
Those scales are ours to cherish
Our rules and laws succumb
To only the best of our own knowledge
And time and space are ours, he'd probably say

Though looking out across this bay, we must
Try a maiden voyage, Icarus, as no locks or cells
Can stay for long, and a kind of grace is on our side
As with my mind there is a wonder that loopholes
I can make from vision and escape when sun prevails
To fly from rank derision.

Beck and Call

The men Daddy D wants to escape
Is an excuse for his art, he
Seeks to do what his art
Allows at all times —
Imagine, engineer, tinker
Until reality conforms,
Snaps to, his invention
Of laws, of arts unheard of

And even this does
Not occur soon enough
Before his imagination
Is taken as hostage
Practical gods, demons
Speaking Greek in his inner ear

And in my home, unsuspecting
A feather comes from some collision
Outside, a flight from a bird of a kind
That loves its young supernaturally, pecks,
Has special features,
It lands and fingering its Velcro,
Ruminates

The bird's distinguishing tracks, its bobbing
Head, quick bug-eating beak. . .

He forgets classification, tradition, the way a world
Works offshore, waves combine, separate — forgets
It all to consider, no to divine
This crisp hatching idea — leaking out
Deftly through each tarsal, feather-brained bone, yet
In perfect geometries, each plume smoothed according to the scale
Of his need in mind's beck and call

My Television

Is located on a mahogany desk my father built
Just like that toy portable garage made into a metal toolcase
When I was five, I took on trips to relieve boredom.

The desk is also used to study flight; books of aeronautics
Bernoulli effect, updraughts, feather structures, bird parts. . .

A wrecking yard of birds and sitcoms
For my attention must span more than wings

Evil Knievel's

My hero, adrenalin
Drives his need to be airborne

Vodka-filled cane, studded knob,
He'd jump the world again and again

Canyons, abysses, chasms
Are his deepest desires

To leap their wide-mouthed faith

Though bones all ramshackled
And knit unevenly

A force, you could say, uncontrolled
Moves him to rev across the air

Let go of a rooted and sugar-almond limelight
One earth, he figures, and a daredevil's need

To repel high windows' submission
To a staid life, instead bust through the panes

Choreographed

Onto another higher roof
In fact to fly, without romantic need

Beyond whatever price is paid
A sort of love, dysfunctional, it is obvious

He comes crashing down, skidding metal engine
And leather shoulders, leggings, elbows

Skip and dance, tossed raggedy-ann
Through the gas-licked flames to rest

Motionless

Then again, and crazy again, begin to write
Lonely for air.

It is Partly Vaudeville

To imagine a man using wings
Like a god, flapping mindlessly
So he could fall flat

I build myself up; pecs, abs, tri- and bi-ceps
So I could meet a rocky ledge and with a grand
Gesture launch this rippling body into Mediterranean air
All my schoolfriends, girlfriends
Await liftoff as father counts backward
From ten. . .

I wanted to fly back then as well, a kid
Imagining from our balcony what soaring
Was like, I'd smile and not know why

Five. . . four. . .
And feel burning calves
Like icebergs, mountains of ice
Falling into a sea burning

Only creative visualization, soaring
Up and away shoulders, arms searching
For updraughts, for respite from an initial
Burn and sputtering, dip and rise

You can't be serious, all this prepping, dreaming,
Plans, fatherly love and all

Two. . . one. . .
Belly-flops into a deep feather bed of cold sea,
Those magic cheerleaders with exposed bellybuttons
Hearing them before I hit on a shore
Having rib-splitting laughs.

White blossoms of sound and plash fade beneath.

We

Happen to be here again
And I cannot say what I want
Because constraints, serial
Learning have portrayed me to be
A citified lover in a minimalist home

And this country is cold
And has critics of the cold
Who live in mountains
Curled in cabins like bobcats
And proclaim the cold theirs
And what makes them different
Is the clear cold in which they express themselves
Of course, like no other, or
It's prairie ghosts that vacate the big sky
Or make under the counter drugs fulfill
A moment's movement along the winding coast
Full of hideaway isles

We happen to be here again
Simply because of constraints
A minimalist lover in a citified home

An unused contraption of wings
On a kitchen chair

Proof

Next to each miniscule motion, notion
Is the miniscule red line of death

Though so far he's operated well
Building, engineering on demand

He stitches, glues and has stabbed
Himself once or twice, a rough needle

Letting it go unnoticed, a thread of red
Spills like crazy stitching across

A wing —
The angle of which is equivalent
To a speeding neuron's immediacy, the greater
The speed, the less the angle, until necessity
Precludes any recognition of blood or angles

And therefore remains entranced in work, dawn to dusk
The sphere of love right next to the sphere of death, he
Listens to what his hands do, gluing, hammering, typing, and
Does so until his work joins body and mind to fly

Icarus Smells

Perfumed wax, lavender, lilac, like barber's cologne
That rubs a face and swirls up behind the ears —
When his father cut his hair it was highly nutritious
His heart rested in open air feeding on a kind of worship
Icarus, head down as sharpness cleared his neck of filoplumes
His father moulds his feathery crown, aerodynamic

Icarus is looking for words to say
But is shaved clean, presentable for gods
Full of an everlasting joy

I Must Be on Something

I have dreams now of stopping under branches
Ruffling and billing almost endlessly —
That fragrance of wings, feathers, dusty hearts
Bring me anywhere and nowhere

Sleepless with all this soaring and swinging in wilderness
Flying in a bird's memory, weightless straps and wings

To believe the old man
All these years heir to his debt
Of art for kings and fancy dreams
And now this — flying
Like some yellow jacket or jay
Escape Crete for him and he wants
Me to lean on his song out of love
Abet him to build a narrative of escape

Kill This (Daedalus Wants Out)

Losing stride, I need to return home, to Naples' rocks
And isles, sultry bandits, low-rent dives, smoke
And volcanic ash, serpentine abodes
Alexandrine shine that undulates onshore

A field day of unconfined skies, blue rambunctious waves
Kill this road to prison in my backyard
Give me the invisible sceptre my mind's eye
Grasps, a kingdom to escape to, mine own,
And watch the birds shape heaven

If We Were in Any Other Time

We'd be lifers in San Quentin, Alcatraz
Sun off our mad bicep tattoos
Morbid mongrels plan our lobotomies

Captains of industry run full tilt with
Monstrous alarms around their mansions
Fearing our needy molls, Daedalus and son

Our sailor vocabulary in a hurricane and
Our intuition, the back-breaking variety.
We escape over the scene, like grinning archangels.

But in a real world we'd be schooled for banishment
Run out of saliva spitting in their faces.
Our conscience would have no remote trace

Our dice shivering under freeze-frame waves
Skeleton keys jangling from our sex slaves
Electroconvulsive skies' constant lightning

Only to find after ditching our wings
We'd be shaped like memories of those gods we knew.

Collect

Feathers, the best
For my hands, order
Filoplumes first, then larger ones laid
Further down the contraption, they must be light
As ghosts for none of this matters
We can live without this island cell
It is illusion, a tease, a lie
Children bathing in a sea, ships and
Houses are garbage, all rubble and smoke,
You saw how implosions reduce wonder
Blood and flesh and stone to smoke and dust
It all disintegrates
Before your eyes to nothing
What further proof do you need?
So, let's go
Collect feathers
Stop watching the ships, their sails
In white luffs
This island we're on
Is nothing more than dust
And you will see at once
We're above it all

True Renderings

In his arid room Icarus guides his nib
to uncharted waters, black indelible pixels
as if on the universe's edge he relays back
drawings on papyrus, an unfaltering audacity
his father knows nothing of.

He draws his dream of angels festooned around a ladder
lucent as they pass each other on rungs
he draws them wondering why they
climb to heaven and descend with
wings he could never dream of using.

14/03

Icarus draws the barmaid, her naked hip
a small pool of moonlight, a stir, like
strains of a feather across his heart—
then smells a steel substrate
a cold integrity, like his father,
or at least his presence swarming around.

06/08

He sketches fishermen onshore
irongall nets spill, thrown to trawl
into a carmine dusk, and transitive
gleaming
low-flying crows
in india ink, wayfarers
still wet from rain
still arriving.

17/10

Icarus Fresh and Brilliant

Finds nothing on TV, his Great Daddy fixing
The airstream across his wings in another room
It is brilliant outside and he gets a whiff of lilac
Or lavender, a familiar aroma and places it —
Barber's cologne that splashes and pats the cheeks
Swirls up behind the ears when Great Daddy's done
With him in the swivel chair
And his neck is clear of filoplumes, his crown swept
Back like feathers, sculpted for wind

Icarus Returns

And presses more numbers on the black remote
The Learning Channel, the Discovery Channel . . .
His vertebrae ache and he senses the pain over
Each of them like blue water subsuming smooth rocks
He sinks further into the deep leather chair his father gave him
It supports his back, his vertebrae learn to breathe underwater.

He settles on *Junkyard Wars.* The teams are to build a flying machine
From scattered remains of accidental engines, disengaged power trains
Wings shot down over fields in heavy rain.
They have eight hours. It is a new idea, a pilot project
To begin a new season.

Meanwhile

His father builds his Pegasus in a workshed
Always reminded of Heisenberg's principle, that
There is always something that cannot be accounted for
In a mind's image or actual fact; missing information
In sketches, the velocity of rumours, rocks exhaling updraughts
And so on, as if in a collision of larks and bears in a field;
A maelstrom of feathers and fur and he misses a nuance —
A motion so crucial it could save homecoming queens' deaths
And if merely noticed, calculated into an equation
Allow the births of Christs to recur

Still he works confident and with iridescent heart
Giving birth, licks each feather carefully before culled
And placed rightfully in a pattern as a kind of kiss
For his son. He imagines Icarus flapping in an even, strong
Rhythm, wings meeting on a downstroke as if praying,
Flying over archetypal isles with infinite ease.

Chronological Order

Icarus hangs out.
Goes for a swim in the cerulean.
Bandages himself. Rocks cut his feet.
Watches stars and birds
Watches TV. Goes out for a walk.
Visits the atelier. His father
Is on pouring wax, its scent
Appeals to Icarus.
His plan is to wait for his father
To finish the wings. He writes daily.
He smokes leaves, the ephedra
Flushes him into stars.
Icarus builds a fire on the beach at night
Sparks pop into starless moonshine
He sits propped by a tree trunk
He is visited by a stray dog that
Falls asleep on his lap.
Icarus sleeps as well and dreams
He is skywriting, moonlight reflects in the dog's eyes,
Giving him reason to howl.

Icarus' Television

Is located on a large mahogany desk
He uses to study flight on
An engineering hopeful, aeronautical —
The world falls for engineers, always in demand
He thinks and smells his roomful of dusty feathers

He feels he is falling, drowning in his father's ocean

His room
A junkyard, wrecking yard of all types of feathers
For the sorting; feathers and fathers

And he imagines a possible scene:
On a mountain cliff, actually, an active volcano's lip
He dons his father's invention
And cannot tell whether he is joyous
Or a sacrifice —
Whether freedom or imminent death looms
Still an exuberant fear as he believes
His father is flight, a bony bald god with wrinkled
Timeless words mixed with rage and dead reckoning love
Some days leads a donkey cart down a mountainside
Full of leather, metal, feathers and others sit
Staring at the horizon as if his life hangs by a thread
And then the father who cuts his hair overlooking the sea
Hearing only slips of scissors snip in spurts
And the hair that floats onto his bib
And he smiles like an antidote

His suffering mother, jackdaw school friends,
A brindle dog, a few idyllic friends
And other characters, birds, relatives, angels (mostly invisible)
And of course the island with trees, rustic mountains and streams, are there

But his father's the one with history, the one that pushes him
Off the brink, smiling, saying
Fly, you wonderful son of a bitch, fly!

Icarus Redux

Icarus senses he's an instrument of his father's
Divine art and love
That is shaped like a problem
His father will solve dreaming, unmoored
From earth by machines
As a result, Icarus won't have time for barmaids
Or getting drunk with warriors
To recite high poems in love
Or attain those women
In shampoo or beer commercials

Instead he rises
To pick through the rocky tongues
Of a shoreline picking feathers
Pelican, gull, tern

Some days he hurries the process
And captures the odd bird dawdling
Wringing its neck above its flailing wings
And feet

Now he keeps both eyes on such birds
And has stopped turning away

From Up Here

We train our high superordinate selves to put you
Through the hoops of savants past, when
Alive maintained a thought, a prosody so high
And simple, the world was held in a grain, a gnat

So from here we see you as beetles roll
Your dung below, so many words like snow
Mixed to make thoughts melt with scat
A baser style of words and too much primacy
Though electric, eclectic, we leave you with that

Above the Water

How could I be any nearer the afternoon blaze?
A sun hums so near
It fishes, drops rays into the sea, like lines
Those shipyards are full of railings
Containers stocked and stacked in meditation
Water turns a certain time without a watch
Always a fitting dark blue,
I cast a burning shadow over burning waves

Energy depletes itself
Thinking of sun in perpetual use
A bright heat over topographies, buried
In geologies, physiologies
Stokes these wings in strokes, and
Sudden updraught glide to see

Crows, black majesties shaken
From a desert, their gleaming breasts
Tin can cracking beaks
Pilgrim strut and
Primordial glare

They begin to circle a field below
Skimming cypresses, then land
Near margins in shade
Brilliant wayfarers, still gleaming

But
No joining them, no rest

Fueled by bright, smouldering wings.

Ursa Major

What are these dragons coiled in me?
Awakened now? Why now? Why midstream?
Pop solicits the lead, a careful
Glance back intermittent between his flapping
And I'm gone to mountaintops and pioneer
Air with his machinery, my chance to speed
Unhinged, take the family car for a joyride
A flying ace
A Boeing or Lear jet
Seek the blonde's heat or lose
Fly so close and high
So I can at least, at last, lust
Before I turn to memory and die

Pallas and Perdix

I guessed as soon as
  Halfway down 32 feet per second
That rocky face flying into my eyes
  Then suddenly an extra lift, eminent doctoral
Wings, feathers in a nanosecond from flailing arms
  Exhaling from this exceptional dream
Featherweight, hard beak
  Ribcage turned hollow, hallowed, two feet ticklish
Pigeon toes, and where the rocks wash
  Into a sea, I can see them lift away, uncollapse
From these lungs that are breathing light normally
  And gladdened eyes, pull away, above the boughs, houses
That man, Daedalus, skulking back into his house from the precipice
  Of his dreadful disfigured shove, the only snake
In this bucolic scene.

And then the future
  Made of atom-smashers, accelerators into light, stealth
Thrushes manned and unmanned, black under radar
  At night, flying over rivers mountains filled with bird varieties
And flowers — who makes us achromatic, asymptomatic with stealth?
  Who is responsible for underhanded guiltless snickerers who love
Those blooming patches of violets, who throw lavender kisses to children
  While unlocking bomb bay doors, unquestioning?

The Shepherd

Like a woolly steamer trunk on its end
Beneath a shady tulip tree, crook in hand
A stocky shepherd watches a flock file past some puddles
Reflecting sky, them, and me. Some
Baying here and there, hardly notices the dream
That sputters plummets, splashes down before
You can say Brueghel the Elder, or Wystan Hugh Auden
Or Harvey Silverstein.

Winging It

Feathers scattered along a rocky shore
Are as natural as an abandoned car
On cinder blocks, sun batters off the hood
Dents are natural like the dirt
Ground into barbicels — a dashboard split
Open with featherfibre, white wavers in a
Microbreeze — I sponge the moment that
Punctures time's flowing with time-consuming
Thought and equals as many
Shimmering waves seen from the corner
Of my eye, by the thousands as barbicels
Crosshatch to catch
A microbreeze in a second's blaze from
Sunlight that coats feathers, rust and hubcaps
All at once, lifts

If truth, or even beauty, lies
Abandoned in any one assembly line object
Colour still bleaches from it, yet
Feathers are somnolent white
Nature bred for quills and upholstery
Or flaming black, or genetic grey, brown
Goes down to the bone mantle
Hopping about on air, hollow light
Dumb as waves battering savage hulls
Their vain rust, like flesh, like roofs and spires
All at once, lifts

Ending Up

In a hospital room, all white
Panic-stricken sheets taut as wood
Disembodied words of Greek surgeons
Outside the white curtain drawn
Half surrounding my bed, 'insane' 'flying'
'jumped off a cliff in Crete'

What could they know, my convocation
Came alone, my wings were blind things
My father made as instruments he showed me
How to use outside my cell window
Winnowing the air?

As now, seeing him outside this semi-private window
10 floors up, mocks my injuries with his
Birdlike glare and swoop and glide
Soliciting again, as if I were with him there

See him even in my dreams, soaring above
Unsettling hi-wave rhythms, calm as you please

This antiseptic hospital smell is putrid and sickens me
The exit staircase not far away.

Though he sent me dying flowers.

Epitaph

Father buries me
Face up —
Birds clean and comb me
They pull a blanket of earth up to my chin
At night

A stepladder allows me to climb out
Into timeless days; hours and minutes elapse
Blue then black
Everyone taking quick steps
Passing before me like wedding guests

Or running to make ransom payments
For their children alive and well
With growing hearts and longing
For their futures

Now and Elsewhere

Despite All Intentions and Appearances These Days

it's simply that most deny
basic life under overturned rock
or grimy roots of a tree
that oozes limbic and wonder there to see
rather they mind their cars, contrive care
that bounds toward pleasure after pleasure
in all possible demeanors our ruby red loves show
how fast we go to laugh and avoid any squeamish measure

so everyday beside unborn bombs we pray
for life and limb to stay just the way they're meant

solid lives with health, wealth and being free
one whole smiling being and not overworry
of other perspectives and the truth
such wondering could bring to light
is the mindful worldly way to live in
yet to die is to recognize
another paradise
beyond the eyes we're given

Milton's Cottage, Chalfont-St.Giles

It has to do with leaning into things
Particular phrases suggest
Themselves from somewhere that appears
Closer to a subject than time itself,
Enters the heart's count and noncount, its
Pulp and meaning alike rummaging together.
Maybe the way he thought more and more
About angels, trying to speak like them
Days he didn't wish to hear them
Were most important, when trumpets
Kept him awake and spoke Aramaic, Greek, Latin
Angelic monkeys on his brain, yelping and singing
Sweet recurrent songs and handing him lines.
So he wakes up his wife, Elizabeth to dictate
More of his paradisial hell as she listens without sleep.
In her eyes he is blind as the south wall
As he articulates some
Ancient angel's scroll of insightful words and words
Keep coming from what he is hearing
In blessed vocation into early morning as republican yells
Break over the hill on his land
With lances and breach-loaders firing off,
Smoke rises from their muzzles and still transfixed he continues
To belt out words to his scribe as she by now could hear
That what she puts down in his meters are the cries amplified
A war's mechanics, satanic yells, pumped with
Clattering blows and God only knows what else, she thought, his
Blindness was miraculously devising.

Horace

Awakening from sleep
    a flickering room in a combo
of dream and sunlight between leaves

    it could be Horace waking on his Sabine farm
Italian light burgeoning through a few rattling branches

    a lucent morning, lambent,
everything prepared to launch into communion

    songs, positively of another dimension that notifies
gaps between colours, an illusory score cannot
    escape the wonder and mystery of what we are

children who throw together a play behind see-through
    blankets, silhouettes acting out dreams from the night before
a boast of mankind as parents brave some anthropomorphic point

with laughter, hoping sons and daughters will come through
    alive, receive the plaudits they deserve, prosper, procreate
and leave behind
    the farm, the trees, a better state of humanity to engage in
like reading about Horace and his honourable ideas, which
    have now gone to waste, but at least engaging, though
only a fragment

as this stay,
    an experience that will end of its own accord

Paz

I.

In a universalistic church,
a choir prepares in the wings
as reading a review
a memoriam to Octavio Paz
articulate voice in political wrecks
leads me to believe once again
as they emerge and begin to sing
sweetly in merry-go-round measures
of Nashe and Campion among flowers
and bees

Meanwhile
a child cries, mother
removes him to the vestibule
to mete out juice
from her blue backpack
and the songs change to Chinese
love songs on a shore
under a China blue sky

In Mesoamerica, Paz writes
finding Mexican landscapes
a valley's ancient flames
that sing wholehearted
sings and sings
stirs up flames of sentiment

2.

...all that is evil in the human mind is contained as a predisposition.
Sigmund Freud

Predisposed to evil
you do not retreat
but knock harder
on the door
then stamp
your jackboots
like spades
storm-shocker who
awakens casual dreams,
to drag
down stairs winding
like water through a rusted drain
by the hair
following the balustrade's black
curve to the stadium outside
under floodlights' glare
opening fire

3.

There is an insurrection that occurs
inward
with common substances like stone
and wood
thrown through windows, cars set
afire
lashing past inches from heart and mind
for freedom
to have dogs and children in open air
lick candy
for satisfaction's release and have
your child
ride the dog and the dog remain speechless
harassed by impending dark

Urobos Codex

And it occurs to me that this is what a writer does to transcend the limitations of his background. He does it through language, obviously. He writes himself into the larger world... He opens himself to the entire culture.

Don DeLillo

Deadbeat factory life, dear god

As if
Returned from some Trojan war,
To find canned tuna and spaghetti
As Boeings lift, aloft, aerospace marvels
Thrust into enlightenment. I mind the kitchen as
Thoughts of Mount Pleasant, an exploded view
Of a Cord. Its pieces painted and glued.
Garments swirl, unrolled material, swaths
From Bombay, spices still linger
O, Noumea, your fibres strewn from sun
Brands of beauty and laughter terrorize
Unknown republics with Salvation Army
Off-the-rack raincoats. Flora leaves for
Fauna, the Montclair Lawn Bowling
Society's annual jaunt to Patagonia
Has wings, hasn't it?
'Sketches of Spain' plays
Epiphanies, where are they going?
You are heaven-sent. Historical singer
Tragedy and comedy embrace
On the Cabot Trail, my hearing impaired
Around Meat Cove, we danced on devonite
At Peggy's Cove, dusklight, ocean lover
It's hard to conceive, isn't it?

Look for subject matter like life
At this juncture we devise, wing it
And revise with more spontaneity
Preview our asphyxiation in future
Routines until unwittingly mortal
We succumb to what we hope is
An afterlife. I take what is given
And at any rate provide imagination
With wonder, and as much as possible
Taking time out for a date or two

O, St. Lucy, Lucy
Divine at the bad breast. Will
Knew the testicles to be eyes, and your
Eyes an offering on a silver platter to God
To circumvent any man's lust and love
Metapsychotic lover! Lucy funny as ever
Grape squeezer, *I Love Lucy* on TV
On silver screen, see me as I see you
Scheme to gain an equality, an equanimity
As it rains outside, red-headed Handel plays for kings
REX VIVAT, fireworks illuminate captivity
On stereophonic walls. The minimalist in me
Is not dead yet. A meteor impact of deadly proportion

Forces a readaption to surroundings and culminates

Infinite regressions rippling out and in.

Clarion Call

Walking into a field
centuries read the earth

their extended blaze
up the long white road
saying all I wanted to say

was, until I die.

Belief

Neruda signs false documents
for the killer of Trotsky
a unique and simple black cursive
across watermarked paper
done hundreds of times near mindless
no less poetic, a duty
coda to poems of others dying
in love-clasps
clapping at book launches in Santiago
his signature stings a title page

as the icepick enters
another history, another life

Hollywood Prayer

Love is a miracle pain
and your dream of Jacob's ladder
takes into account the umbilical chords of Jericho
where endings slip through endings, walls and
walls crack and your hair ignites across Naugahyde
in your film, you decide on beauty, who has it
who doesn't with the ruthless power of a stranger
and what car takes us across Death Valley is your choice
or where the pools of genes will lie in mansions as
iridescent dreams convert to huge salaries
paid for in diamond cocktails, reimbursed
for a sun that tans your pain
dulcimer touch of your mind expands its song
once a day at least to take rhythms of your arching back
to universal studios of thought and mystical lovers like
a swallow's roulette spin and dart until
nothing goes and the thought of a gun's acrimony sinks
to a sadness about you and still
California light pours in a bay window
waves splash unwritten across rocks and poetry
you believe to be true as time
is spent on wondering
about indulgences of every kind.

(Lord, come down to me alone
I am more sinned against than sinning
these homes are houses you built
as well and I cannot be blamed
for your automatic reasons, your tenuous love
bleeds gifts for me, O Krishna, Buddha, Allah
dream me from your constellations in a cosmic sky
days I cried and having sent you prayers, their diamond-cut
words is all I can do from here in character
in this house where I re-enact your covenant
I am poor as my companions are rich
their parents toiled to leave poverty

behind in wars and famine's bones
Lord these are the empties I've not cashed in
their worth is your command
and these masks are a cinematographer's direction
days I cried along Rodeo Drive and felt
ill winds blow through these empty eye sockets
as if I hung from a tree — or drive my Viper —
with little knowledge swing one way and another
free in a wind, finally, down Rodeo Drive)

Ovid by the Black Sea

In remarkable lives many gaze at the sensual
the abusive and still fall under spells of wonder
at the audacity of genius' contribution to
our reflective world, our mirrored world
yet poets riddle old works for clues
to nail down their inspiration and have
some plausible insight to how this
worked so well

He walks the trails of Tsarskoye Selo
remarkable garden walks with thoughts and
haunting barbs no doubt, still his footprints
draft great poems under dark olive leaves

Priests in canticles subsume his greatness
though outcast, his body anoints transgressions,
what an exile! To roam lush aromas, speaking
easily to himself of deities' grace and wars
as waves transact the sea, a critical mass
of words, moonlit, delicate hairs
of the forearm, nape

Ice at Noon, the Dance

Captured here, a mediocre café in winter
          a sun dances gleaming over wiry ice
and trees outside, though
          this could be a means to recognize how
impelling nature can be:
          brightness burning an illumined and lovely world

          but musicians play sounding second rate
unspoiled, unrefined
          made appealing at the sight
of this short middle-aged woman, compact, stout
          who begins to dance with a tall, handsome young man

firmly her hand on his shoulder
          she begins to move lightly, her bright smile
in his dark eyes, they move like poignant hopeful figures through
          dank, listless air
compelling warmth in their motions issues
          a grace like light on ice, radiates,
impinges a sad possibility, a missing point to it all
          though no revelation, simply

how a world beyond this sits in a man-made mediocrity
          and disappointment subsides many into resignation
but here
          in times such as these, can show us, lovely, how
we could be, light in noonday winter
          blazes with them dancing off icy trees

On the Morning News, Live from a Heliocopter

High time to leave this high life
at 140 mph, turn off the highway
having side-swiped slower cars
speeding up, dismantled
ecstasy's soft shoulders, reinvented
this city, strip mined to asphalt
Neruda, my brother, rise up with me
speed
your surrealist pipeline
from the bottom of oceanic love
Machu Picchu regenerates
proper nouns and the Aztec air
silent with death and balance
ritualized heaven's jaguars
I pass at lightspeed defy
the scaffold that built the marvel
death inside me folds and refolds
going nowhere fast, faster, blood
clouds, those sirens
calling from depths speak to me
from the sun that I aim for,
I've trained long to suffer, stellar
centuries as wind, a magnet
anchored to you and wanting to launch
timeless knowing no outcome
my 15 minutes are up, wanting
a manic dissolve to hasten my words
blood
tornado, full-tilt semi, Neruda
breaks into relief and lightning.

Water boils to high-pitched whispers
at the edge of the kitchen, like sonnets
against rocks of Puente Norte, spumes.

Amygdala

So inconsiderate
that this limbic system, venerable
beady-eyed, Hamlet killer, father
slayer over thousands of centuries
housed in dark recess,
holds the secret
to war and anger
spoils a perfect day out

struck you as odd
because there was no excuse
no word to ward off
an assault, neuron starbursts
batter beautifully along
pathways to closed fist's unconscious blow

so inconsiderate
as to border another time, place
a fight or flight reaction to heathen threat
a sabre-toothed grin that snaps open thoughtless
firing sparks in a cave;
gyrus fornicatus, uncus, hippocampus
regions unknown until latin-brained
surgeons opened
the thoughtless stuff

and my remorse assuaged again
by your words of how human
and forgivable it is
and yes, divine (God engenders fatal
wrath to resolve hate, you said) to strike
and now we are closer than ever
my shining love around your eye
your timely stretch of imagination
a wonderful cut, white to the bone, undying

Paying Youth No Mind

Your transient hunger
    on the street
your distended shape
    lasts longer
in afterimage as words
    question our
guilt-spun audacity
    to mourn
a crooner's full celebrity life
    than your cramped
small fingers, stiff ponytail
    fresh ankle

Our aging humanity desires
    humid nights in
love and lust, you had
    no chance to make
anything, passion, blood
    reaching deepest cells
on king/queensize beds
    bearing had no use
the land itself anchored
    your footsteps
leviathan world
    fleshing out breath
intoning whisper
    a dead language
with the least objections
    to your passing.

At Home in the World: A Bluestreak

1.

Aurelius says time is short
and he should know, shouldn't he?
Not being better than others, like
Lao-Tzu, yielding like water to
the grace of time

Stoic Australian crawl, steady
plod under a soaring sun
in a hammock hearing
fixtures screwed
into the bark, squeak
rhythmically,
in these wooden parts
the sounds could be
Myrrha and Cinyrus

2.

Ah, great books are getting
cheaper like great heroes
their lives deconstructed
to lust and to write a great
book now along the lines
of Homer with Bosnia, Rwanda
Omagh, Nairobi, Dar es Salaam
and many others where panic
grounds memory to heinous dust
belittles any noble cause
and still our skies remain
blue in cosmic weather
fostered in our psychotic
beauty even as we speak or as
our hindquarters stirred to stand and
bathwater overflowed in Archimedean

eurekas! or an ocean moors and laps
an autumn in St. Lucia for a poet
as young mouths in timeless fashion
display their sex, wave after wave
disarm and grieve from innocence to grave
it simply is, yet how can we accept simplicity
since in medias res we come expected from birth
to understand history, geology and time itself as joy
which some of us do, as if sifting through

smithereens washed ashore, and then link into perspective
Man's jumbo ego hard-wired to invention
but with a shrimp of a soul
from conception to his dawning neo-cortical arousal
believing the largest lies about himself
while a Lazarus bears witness
to miracles and exists for others
and goes by numerous names
unheeded except for the weak and tawdry

3.

You are aware this is a long lie
as I pull a newspaper from its polyethylene
cover, rain echoes its undoing, columns
with facile politics, petroleum run amok
taking serious advantage of this sort of
utopia slash paradise slash earth
there is little place to go from here
that is advisable let alone livable
though we enjoy movement intensely;
baseballs, jets, satellites, shuttles, probes
to investigate intergalactic voids
sending back roaring statistics
as geographies live and die

awards for peace are handed out

Shopping for Goods

As the epileptic wheel on the cart
storms its crippled beat
we gather, gather our hearts
in a broken music across
refrigerated pieces priced in heaven

Nothing left, spent
lovers incommunicado
take your essential ingredients,
take this money, this time
providence is a dream no one remembers
any more than you, whom I love
and cannot say as much, but
connive and expose
in marketplaces; Agora, Marakesh, unannounced
my shopping exceeds my grasp, more
than I can chew but strive to apprehend
with eyes, heart, your disciple that hankers
pushing a noisy off-centred cart past
your disapproving gaze
o my parents! o my teachers!

On Seeing Albert Herbert's 'Jesus is Stripped of his Garments', 1987

Old and battered New
Testament endorsed
by FDR, 1942, with wartorn
yellow pages to accentuate
popular hymns, prayers,
and Psalm
23, some soldier, some home fire
rebirth reading
the cool eventual breeze across
foreheads, listening
to gospel voices sing new
fusion, street-soul, this morning
is my shepherd, there are no still
waters, pastures are asphalt, no-fault
delusions abound, I want the music
to restore soul, not fearing evil
hands idle
flipping art pages now, frenetic
twentieth restless, senseless, wondrous century
and they leer, eyes at war tear
your soul from limb to hate, bring
you in line, align you with mortality
crowds deeply disturbed
that would come out knowing your crime
trumped up, fools
but they came and tore at your pulse
to think those eyes, chanting
women's
moved in the feet of antiquity
around altars in chorus or that
same bravery, men's
hearts travelled to
conquer kings
reach democratic wizardry
pounding out poetry
for oars' sure rhythm
a refuge in transcendence
for the wretched
in thee forever, amen.

Taking Pictures

With no religion there is nothing
But paranoia. With taking pictures
I make assertions without
Languishing in denial about what could
Have been included/excluded. I take
Portraits of you where you are or
Where you have been and the backgrounds
Vary from falls to coliseums to state buildings.
Hundreds of heartless pictures will
Feed panoramic albums of nostalgia
Staged joy, ones that ask you to smile
Say "gruyere" and press the shudder.
The rest is stasis, little more than tourist
Stuff, what obviously attracts one to
Poetry
Resides in rhyme and reason for rhyme
Of the greeting bard; hovels, distended
Bellies of children are basslines, righteous
Calls to our helpless conscience.
Whereas calls to assure our immortal being
Rank high as pleasure-speak,
Cults forever generate your spirit
To commune with pleasure, our consumer hearts, never
Consumed by titanic death, a waste
Of time and money to sink to that depth,
Though lyrical and beautifully featured
Rarely do I capture a shining flower
To symbolize beauty.
Yet in seeing them board their
Yellow buses in colourful small smiles
Even children fresh from kissing
Their immortal moms and dads
Must go

And maybe when the acridness
Arrives, flies into innocence, an event
Spikes brains alive and gravitates
Downward, fans out to organs
Down through thighs
To tarsals and heels and struck speechless
By hyacinth or hyacinth girls or a ghostly image
A sermon, a lens that has captured Caliban on the fly.

Now and Elsewhere

Dawn soon rose in the country far from Ithaca
        and clouds lift imagination
respond to diversity and dialects in mahogany repose

there is no wailing in fear (at least not so far)
        no dreaded Charybdis and the portable fan's soft wind
strokes face and forehead, intent less urgent than

setting sail for home, shipmates snapping to order, watch for
        fateful signs from deadly gods,
but, business-like, Telemachus
        and Odysseus return to politeness, decorum, throwing arms
around his great father but rather than cry out
        sharper than vultures' and eagles' shrill remorse, now provide
investment tips, tips untempered in another world though analogies
        work with portfolios, and blue-chip warriors stringing bows.

I suppose it works in a different way
        a Muse's song the call of insight into shares
of technology of solid oxides. But where does the ship lie
        moored that brought you here? Where the Parnassus boar's
sweet scar?

Now, the days are elsewhere,
        filaments, cursive over green country pages
in a distant education.

Matt Santateresa is the author of two books of poetry,
Combustible Light and *A Beggar's Loom*.
He lives and writes in Montreal.